Fingertip Friends
letters and drawings by J.H. Stroschin
lyrics by John Mooy

For Christy
Remember to!
Thank a Vet.!
Jane Stroschin

DEDICATION

The Vietnam war will long remain a living memory. Passed from generation to generation are the stories of those who served their country's request in a tiny place half way around the world.

For over 58,000 young men and women, each filled with everyday emotion, hopes, and dreams, life was simply done too soon.

From the memory of those lives lost must come the commitment and inspiration necessary to resolve conflict peacefully, without loss of life.

This book is dedicated to those who went to Vietnam, those who returned, and those who never did.

J.M. and J.S.

© Stroschin-Mooy
ISBN 1-883960-24-X

Henry Quill Press
Jane Stroschin
7340 Lake Dr.
Fremont, MI 49412-9146

Army Commendation

Purple Heart

Bronze Star

with special thanks to:
David, Gary, Dan, Anita, Al, Sandy,
Richard, and Tom

Arms length wall of stories
carved here in stone,
etched in mad moments
so far from home.

Standing stone silent
so tall and so proud,

18th Engineer Brigade

11th Armored Cavalry Regiment

196th Infantry Brigade

Army Aviator Wings

can't help but feel
you were used up somehow.

Helicopter Flight School
(Above the Best)

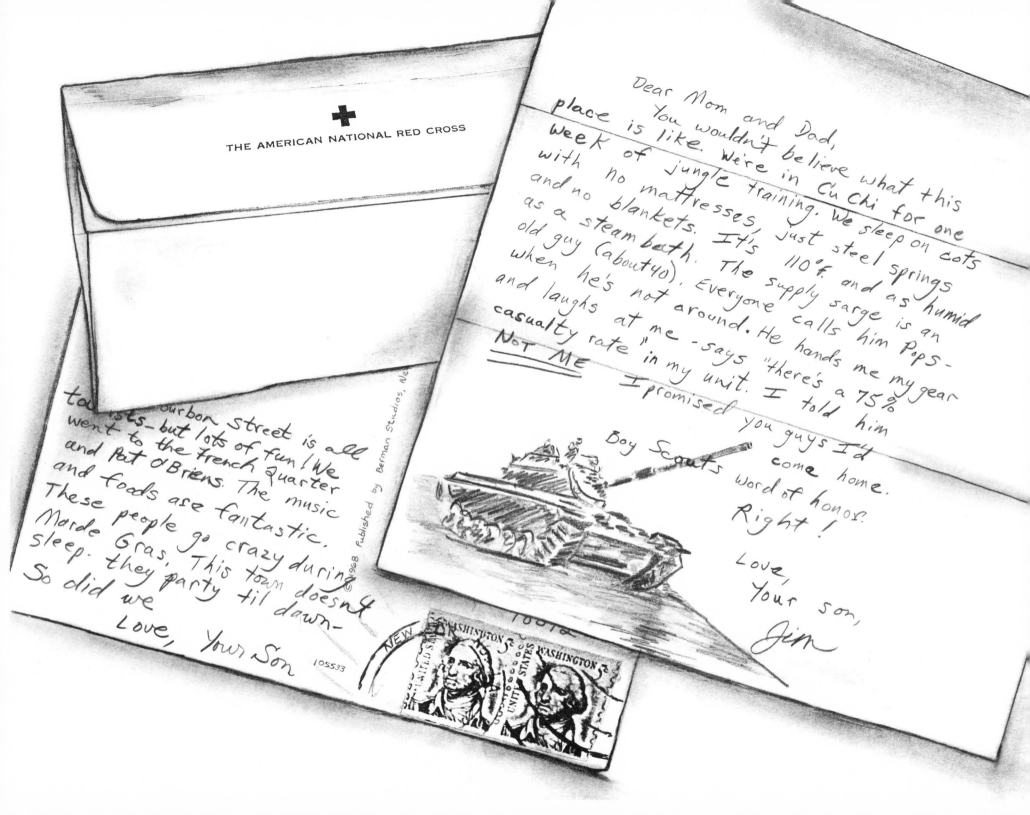

101 st Airborne Division (Airmobile)

Greenfields and mountains,
paddies and clouds,
oh how I miss you
It's not right somehow.

Distinguished Flying Cross

Dear Mom and Dad,

The chopper dumped us and some food supplies in a field where we were greeted by mortar rounds. So we scrambled to a duece½ and headed for camp. It's been quiet ever since. The jungle is lush and green. When you look down at it you can see the red tile roof tops of the villages. The flooded rice paddies go on for miles. The water is so still it reflects a mirror image of the sky. It's hard to tell if you're looking up or down. My "home" is surrounded with barbed wire, land mines and sand bags stacked up to metal covered windows. Wish all this protection kept out the mosquitoes! They're maneaters!

I miss you more than words
        can say
        Love, Jim

P.S. Send Kool-aid and cookies PLEASE

1st Cavalry Division (airmobile)

Though you can't hear me
an arms length away
we call out your names
day after day.

Can you forgive us
as we carry on
reflections say I'm here
the names say you're gone.

Eagle – Boy Scouts of America

My dearest Jimmy —

We watch the news every night on TV, and we pray for you. We thought you'd like these photos. Your "little" brother has gotten taller since the day we said good-bye. And Aunt Agnes thought you'd like to have this photo of Bobby — since you two are like brothers. He drove home for Christmas in the worst snow storm we've had in years. Now he's at Fort Rucker — "Huey" training.

Your Dad has been carrying your Eagle Scout medal in his pocket ever since you left. It's his reminder to pray for you and it reminds him of how proud he is of you.

It seems everyone in town is proud of you. Even cranky Mrs. Jackson, next door, brought you this fudge. But I know your favorites are oatmeal raisin. So here are lots of them — you can share with the boys.

Your Dad is on the phone now bragging about you to Uncle Harry. I'm sure Harry is bragging about Bobby. I love you my sweet angel.

xoxoxo
Mom

A CHEERFUL HELLO

You marched through the madness
a step out of time,
fingertip friends
how you fill up my mind.

Dat's F' de Doids..

U.S. Navy - VC66 Fighter Squadron
WW II

NATIONAL DEFENSE

TACTICAL AIR COMMAND

AIR FORCE F-89 SQUADRON

Hi Family, Happy Birthday Ma! Just wanted to let you know I'm thinking of you on your day. I know everyone at home is praying for me. I can tell- because 3 nights ago Charlie sent us some more mortar rounds. My platoon leader was wounded badly enough to be evacuated-he'll be OK in a few months. Smitty is in the hootch next to mine. He never got a chance to hit the floor. He was in bed sleeping when the shrapnel hit his pet monkey-that was asleep on his chest. The monkey saved his life!

So now we keep flareships up circling our post all night and this keeps ole' Charlie pretty timid about using his mortars because the muzzle flashes are really easy to spot at night.

Dad your WWII stories never meant much to me until now. We were always the handshake sort of guys. But now I really want to make it home - for a lot of reasons- especially because I want to hug you and tell you face to face how much I love you. And how proud I am to be your son.

I salute you Lt. Col. Dad

Love, Jim

Military Assist. Command, Vietnam

Fingertip friends
my hands touch your names,
imagine what you went through
and feeling your pain.

The lessons lay before us
we must learn from the past,
to never allow this
to happen again.

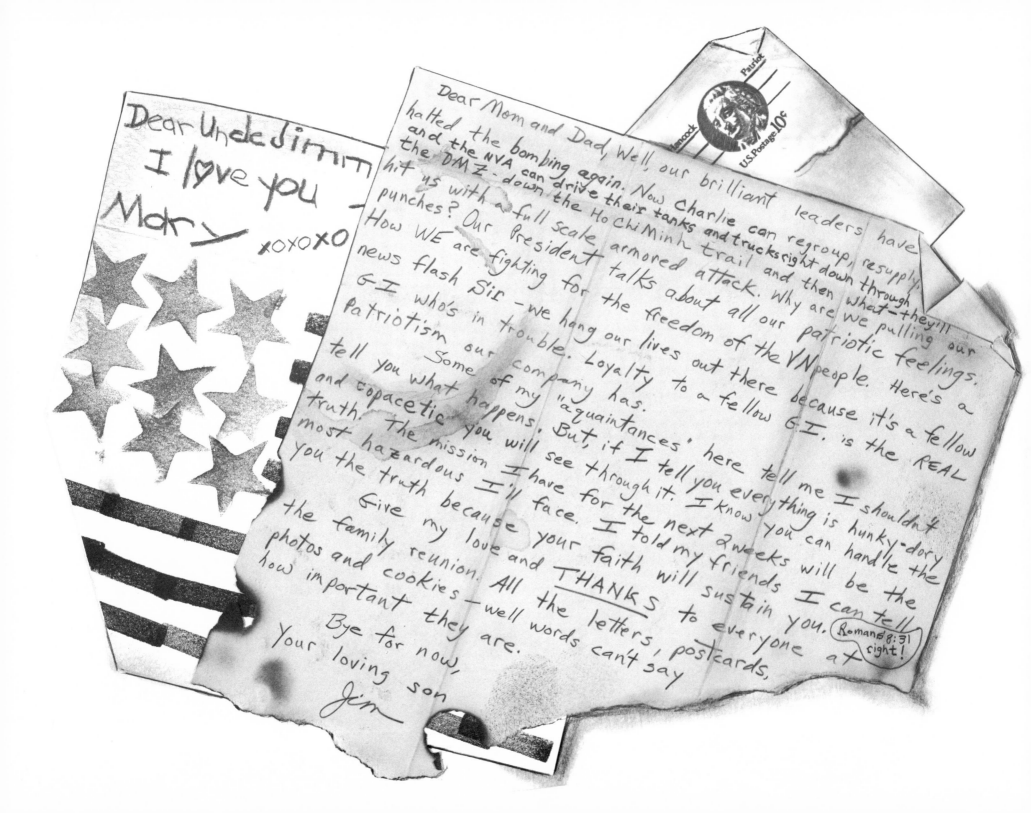

Motionless soldiers
you'll never know
you must believe me
and trust I won't go.

Faces won't fade
when the days drift on by,
you're right here beside me
can you hear my cry?

Your local radio announcement <u>really</u> worked.

P.S., Oh Mother— I got the supplies for the orphans from your friends. Toothpaste, brushes, soap, paper tablets, garden seeds, crayons, pencils and lots more. I'll go to Sister Sarah Paul's school tomorrow to deliver it all. The children are so sad, and beautiful, and so innocently trapped in all this.

Guess who came to visit! I didn't get to see him—I got guard duty. So I get a 3 day pass.

Sorry about this paper—it's all I've got for now.

Medal of Honor
Navy, Marine Corps

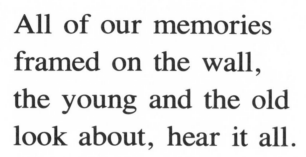

Air Medal

All of our memories
framed on the wall,
the young and the old
look about, hear it all.

The days you were here
are in numbers too small
you were so brave
to answer the call.

Combat Medical Badge

7th Air Force

Fingertip friends
my hands touch your names,
imagine what you went through
and feeling the pain.

The lessons lay before us
we must learn from the past
to never allow this
to happen again.

199th Infantry Brigade
(Medical specialists)

Dear Mom and Dad, As I wake up from one more surgery - who do you think is standing next to my bed - JOHN WAYNE !

He asked me about my wounds so I told him about the sniper came up from a spider hole while we were on patrol BLAM BLAM - there goes my hand, arm, and my flak jacket becomes part of my chest. The M.A.S.H. doc says I'll loose my hand and probably my arm or face 2yrs. of surgery. So here I am.

Well - the Duke was wearing this white ten gallon hat - a Stetson, with a yellow cord around it. I said," I know that cord - it's Cavalry. My unit was the 4th - a pre-civil war division". He says, "Yeah. Back then it was horses - now it's Tanks. I'll send you a hat."

The doctor said I'm stuck here for A LOT longer. And they sound really good about saving my limbs.

So don't worry

All my love   Jim

P.S. I doubt he'll send the hat

The nurse said she'd write this for me But I said No. I had to prove to you I could do this.

To never allow this,
to never allow this,
to never allow this,
to happen again.

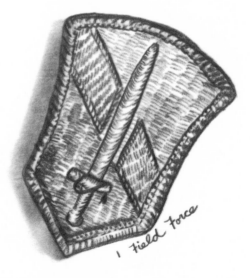

1954	President Eisenhower sends $100 million and U.S. Navy ships to Saigon to support South Vietnam President Diem.
1955	U.S. agrees to train South Vietnam Army.
1961	President Kennedy affirms U.S. support for Laos.
1962	American advisers in South Vietnam number 12,000.
1963	November 2, President Ngo Dinh Diem is killed. November 22, President Kennedy is assassinated. President Johnson ups U.S. support to 15,000 advisers and $500 million in aide.
1964	In late August U.S. bombs North Vietnam.
1965	First U.S. ground troops (Marines) arrive in Da Nong, South Vietnam. December 25, President Johnson proposes a cease-fire.
1966	January 31, U.S. bombing resumes. U.S. troops in Vietnam number 400,000.
1967	General Westmoreland is optimistic that President Johnson and Ho Chi Minh will negotiate peace, once bombing is halted. U.S. troops in Vietnam number 500,000.
1968	January 31, the Tet offensive begins. U.S. troops in Vietnam number 590,000.
1969	Under President Nixon, secret bombing begins in Cambodia. 25,000 U.S. troops withdraw from Vietnam. September 3, Ho Chi Minh dies.
1970	Henry Kissinger begins talks with Le Due Tho. U.S. troops in Vietnam number 280,000.
1971	U.S. troops in Vietnam reduced to 140,000.
1972	North Vietnam attacks, crossing the demilitarized zone. Under President Nixon, U.S. escalates bombing of North Vietnam.
1973	Henry Kissinger and Le Due Tho agree to a cease-fire. U.S. military draft ends. On March 29, the last U.S. troops leave Vietnam.
1975	South Vietnam surrenders.
1982	150,000 people attend the dedication ceremony on Veterans Day in Washington, D.C. of the Vietnam War Memorial.
1994	On Memorial Day, Fingertip Friends is sung at the wall.

Fingertip Friends

Lyrics by John Mooy • Music by Harry Burkstaller • Arranged and mixed by Chris Parks

Arms length wall of stories
carved here in stone,
etched in mad moments
so far from home.

Standing stone silent
so tall and so proud,
can't help but feel
you were used up somehow.

Greenfields and mountains,
paddies and clouds,
oh how I miss you
It's not right somehow.

Though you can't hear me
an arms length away
we call out your names
day after day.

Can you forgive us
as we carry on
reflections say I'm here
the names say you're gone.

You marched through the madness
a step out of time,
fingertip friends
how you fill up my mind.

Fingertip friends
my hands touch your names,
imagine what you went through
and feeling your pain.

The lessons lay before us
we must learn from the past,
to never allow this
to happen again.

Motionless soldiers
you'll never know
you must believe me
and trust I won't go.

Faces won't fade
when the days drift on by,
you're right here beside me
can you hear my cry?

All of our memories
framed on the wall,
the young and the old
look about, hear it all.

The days you were here
are in numbers too small
you were so brave
to answer the call.

Fingertip friends
my hands touch your names,
imagine what you went through
and feeling the pain.

The lessons lay before us
we must learn from the past
to never allow this
to happen again.

To never allow this,
to never allow this,
to never allow this,
to happen again.

Jamie had a BOY!! Love Mom xoxo xoxo

And Dad

Sandy

Marlboro Country

for those who fight for it Freedom has a flavor The protected will never know.

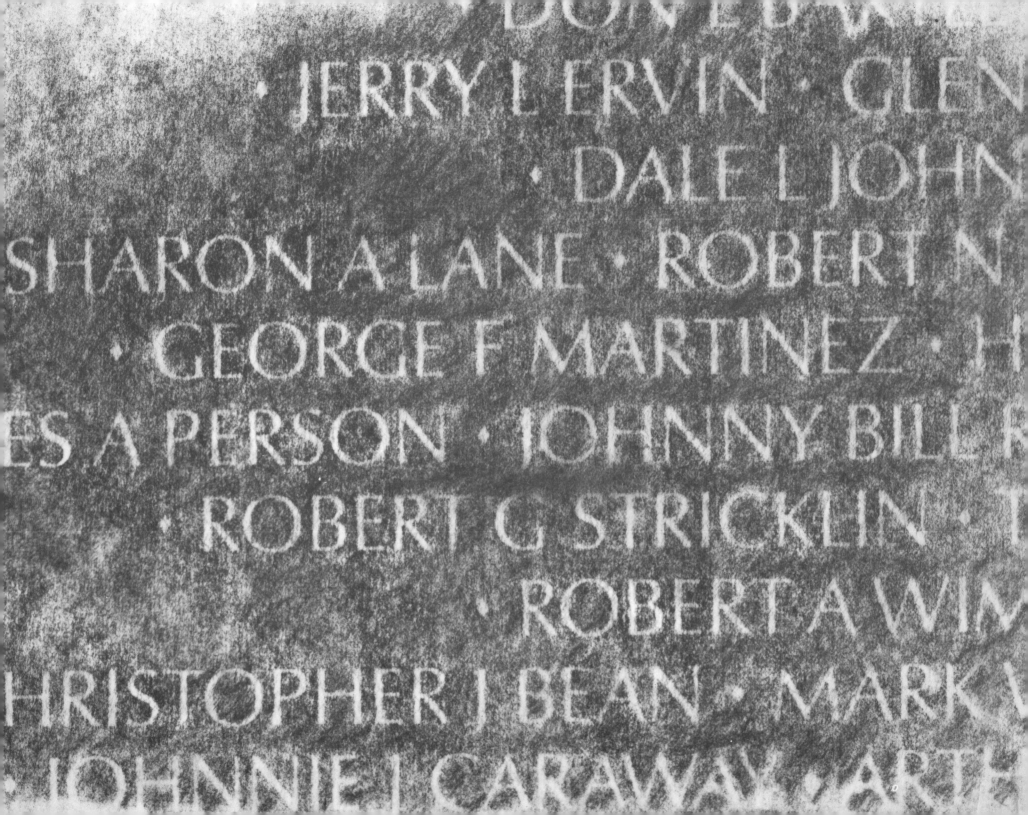

DON E BAKE

• JERRY L ERVIN • GLEN

• DALE L JOHN

SHARON A LANE • ROBERT N

• GEORGE F MARTINEZ • H

ES A PERSON • JOHNNY BILL

• ROBERT G STRICKLIN •

• ROBERT A WIM

HRISTOPHER J BEAN • MARK

JOHNNIE J CARAWAY • ART